COOL SCIENCE

UNUSUAL DISEASES

Michael C. Harris

Marshall Cavendish
Benchmark

New York

Other Marshall Cavendish Offices:
Marshall Cavendish International (Asia) Private Limited, 1 New Industrial Road, Singapore 536196 •
Marshall Cavendish International (Thailand) Co Ltd. 253 Asoke, 12th Flr, Sukhumvit 21 Road, Klongtoey Nua,
Wattana, Bangkok 10110, Thailand • Marshall Cavendish (Malaysia) Sdn Bhd, Times Subang,
Lot 46, Subang Hi-Tech Industrial Park, Batu Tiga, 40000 Shah Alam,
Selangor Darul Ehsan, Malaysia

Marshall Cavendish is a trademark of Times Publishing Limited

Library of Congress Cataloging-in-Publication Data
Harris, Michael C. (Michael Christopher), 1963-
Unusual diseases / Michael C. Harris.
p. cm. — (Cool science)
Includes index.
ISBN 978-1-60870-077-6
1. Rare diseases—Juvenile literature. I. Title.
RC48.8.H37 2011
616—dc22
2009053773

Created by Q2AMedia
Series Editor: Bonnie Dobkin
Art Director: Harleen Mehta
Client Service Manager: Santosh Vasudevan
Project Manager: Kumar Kunal
Line Artist: Vinay Kumar Sharma
Coloring Artist: Nazia Parveen
Photo research: Debabrata Sen
Designers: Cheena Yadav, Parul Gambhir

The photographs in this book are used by permission and through the courtesy of:

Cover: Alexander Raths/Shutterstock, Sgt. Austin M. May/U.S. Air Force
Half title: Mopic/Shutterstock

4-5: Tim Sloan/AFP; 4: M. Dykstra/Shutterstock; 6: Janice Haney Carr/Centers for Disease Control and Prevention; 7: Brasiliao/
Shutterstock; 8: James Robinson/Photolibrary; 9: Miramiska/Shutterstock, Tracy Whiteside/Shutterstock; arlindo/Istockphoto;
10: Centers for Disease Control and Prevention; 11: Sebastian Kaulitzki/Shutterstock; 12: Dea/G. Dagli Orti/Getty images;
13t: Ingor Normann/Shutterstock; 13b: Dea/G. Dagli Orti/Getty images; 14: Kushnirov Avraham/Dreamstime; 15: John Snow
Museum; 16l: Dr. Fred Murphy/Centers for Disease Control and Prevention; 16r: History of Medicine; 17: Dr. Charles Farmer,
Jr./Centers for Disease Control and Prevention; 18: James Gathany/Centers for Disease Control and Prevention; 20: National
Museum of Health and Medicine; 21: Glenbow Archives, Calgary, Canada NA-4548-5; 22: WHO; 23: Hulton Archive/Stringer/
Getty Images; 24: Dr. Lyle Conrad/Centers for Disease Control and Prevention; 25: National Institutes of Health; 26: Liliya Drifan/
Dreamstime; 27: Eric Isselée/Shutterstock; 28: Centers for Disease Control and Prevention; 29: Courtesy of Friends of Joseph
Carey Merrick; 30: Akhtar Soomro/Rex Features; 31: AP Photo; 32: Paul Van Nespen; 33: Janice Carr/Centers for Disease Control
and Prevention; 34: Paul Fleet/Shutterstock; 35: Dermatology Online Journal; 36: Sipa Press/Rex Features; 37: Cathy Trost;
38: Sabina Pierce/AP Photo; 39: Photo courtesy Rick Guidotti and the Moebius Syndrome Foundation; 40: Centers for Disease
Control and Prevention; 41: Sergey Kamshylin/Shutterstock; 42: Centers for Disease Control and Prevention;
44: James Gathany/Centers for Disease Control and Prevention; 45: Dr. Scott Smith/Centers for Disease Control and Prevention

Q2AMedia Art Bank: 19, 43

Printed in Malaysia (T)

1 3 5 6 4 2

CONTENTS

DEADLY DISEASES

Typhoid. Malaria. Smallpox. Diseases such as these have terrified people for centuries. Some are still spreading panic today.

Why? Let's say you catch a cold. At the worst, you have a cough or a stuffed nose, and maybe your muscles ache. You miss a couple days of school, and soon you're as good as new. When it comes to common colds and familiar forms of the flu, our bodies—and sometimes medicine from our **pharmacies**—are all we need to fight the battle.

But there are some diseases that are so different, and sometimes so strange, that neither our bodies nor our doctors and scientists know how to fight them.

DAILY NEWS

SWINE FLU SCARE!

Hundreds of locations across the city dispensing free flu vaccines.

What Is Disease?

A disease is a condition in a living thing, or one of its parts, that stops it from functioning normally. Diseases are caused by **microorganisms**, such as viruses and bacteria; or by a **genetic defect**. Each illness has certain signs, or symptoms. These can be anything from spots on the skin, to a high temperature, to **nausea**.

Some diseases are very rare and hard to treat. Many can permanently cripple people. Some can even lead to death. In fact, extreme cases have killed millions of people around the world. Others affect very few people, but the effects are extreme. Widespread or limited, though, one thing about these unusual diseases is certain. They are all fascinating—and a little bit frightening.

During the H1N1 flu scare in 2009, people lined up for hours to receive vaccines.

Free H1N1 Flu Vaccine

Cuando completando la forma de consentimiento, por favor complete rellenando TODO el círculo.

ejemplo

WHAT CAUSES DISEASE?

Some diseases are hard to understand or cure. But we can usually find the source in one of four groups of suspects: bacteria, viruses, fungi, parasites, and **genetics**. Each group does its damage in a different way.

Bacteria

Bacteria are tiny, single-cell organisms. They are so small that a single grain of soil may contain more than 100 million bacteria! Bacteria live in every habitat, or environment, on Earth. They exist on land, in the air, and in water. They can even live in radioactive waste!

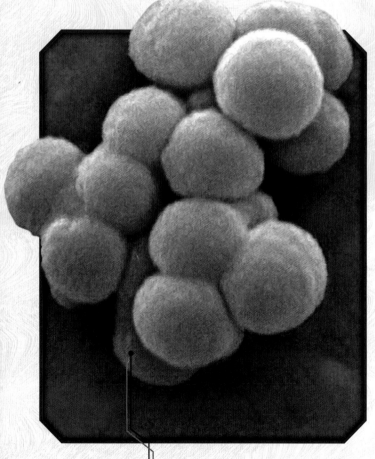

Bacteria are single-cell organisms that may be shaped like rods, spheres, or spirals.

Bacteria can be found on our bodies and in our bodies. Most are harmless to us because our **immune system** protects us. Some bacteria are even helpful. For example, some live in our intestines and help us digest our food.

The most common illnesses caused by bacteria are **respiratory** illnesses—illnesses that have to do with breathing. But there are other more dangerous illnesses we can get from bacteria. For example, we may get a staph infection. Staph, or staphylococcus, is a specific type of bacteria that infects tissues in our bodies.

These bacteria enter the body through a cut and infect the area around the opening. But staph can also infect our lungs, heart, and other organs. One type of pneumonia is caused by staph bacteria, as are most cases of food poisoning.

The risk of staph infections is high in patients who undergo surgery.

Infections are a major problem in hospitals. Because many patients have surgical wounds, the staph bacteria have lots of opportunities to infect people.

The treatment for most staph infections is antibiotics. Antibiotics are drugs that seek out and destroy bacteria in our bodies. For milder bacterial infections, people can take pills containing antibiotics, but for more serious cases, the drug is injected directly into people's veins.

Fungi, Protozoans, and Parasites

Many types of fungi look like plants, but they cannot make their own food. Some live on the skin and can cause **ringworm** and other infections. Others are more serious, causing brain inflammation and lung disease. Protozoans are one-celled organisms. The ones that cause diseases such as **dysentery** and **sleeping sickness** live mainly in tropical areas.

Parasites—which can be fungi and protozoans—are organisms that live in or on animals and feed off them. Humans get parasites from water, from food, and sometimes from their pets. Once they've infected a host, parasites reproduce quickly. In fact, all they do is eat and grow. Some types of parasites can only be viewed with a microscope. Other types are much larger, like tapeworms.

Tapeworms, which are parasites that live in a person's stomach or intestines, can grow to be many feet in length!

Parasites can make humans sick in different ways. For example, lice are parasites that can be found anywhere on the body. Head lice feed on blood from a person's scalp and cause itching. Luckily, they do not lead to illness. Body lice, on the other hand, can spread serious diseases. These lice are usually found in crowded, unsanitary conditions, where people cannot bathe or change clothing regularly.

Trichinosis is another kind of parasitic disease. People can get it from eating certain kinds of meat, like pork, that aren't cooked thoroughly. Trichinosis can make people very sick, sometimes even causing death. Usually it's caught early enough that medication takes care of the problem.

JUST AMAZING!

You would be surprised by how often the organisms hiding in our own food make us sick. That's why storing and preparing foods correctly is so important. Here are a few facts:

- There are more than 200 kinds of different diseases caused by viruses, bacteria, and parasites found in food.
- It has been estimated that 60 percent of the raw poultry sold in stores contains some kind of disease-causing bacteria.
- Cutting boards and kitchen tools that have not been cleaned can spread bacteria from one food to another.

Head lice are a common problem and have nothing to do with personal hygiene. Medication gets rid of them easily.

Viruses

Viruses are sneaky. They're also tiny—up to one thousand times smaller than bacteria. They are not cells, like other parasites or bacteria. They are **molecules**, but like parasites they need a host body in order to reproduce and grow.

Viruses are spread through coughing and sneezing, through water or food, or through contact between people. Many ordinary illnesses are caused by viruses. These include familiar ones like the common cold or seasonal flu, or even cold sores. But some viruses can be deadly. Smallpox, Ebola hemorrhagic fever (EHF), and swine flu are all caused by viruses.

Viruses can mutate and change, which makes it hard for scientists and doctors to cure viral diseases. A cure that works on one form of the virus might not have any effect at all on a mutated version. That's why the treatment for milder viruses like the seasonal influenza virus is usually rest. This gives the body the energy it needs to develop **antibodies** that can fight off the invader. Once our immune system learns to battle that particular virus, it usually can't make us sick again.

A virus consists of a nucleic acid wrapped in a thin coat of protein. Nucleic acids control the functions of living cells.

GENIUS AT WORK

In 1898, a Dutch microbiologist named Martinus Beijerinck posted research proving that something smaller than a bacteria could cause diseases. He learned this while looking for the cause of a disease that stunts tobacco plants. He pressed out the juice of infected tobacco leaves and passed it through a filter that removed bacteria. The juice was still able to infect healthy plants. Because Beijerinck thought the juice itself was the cause of the disease, he called it a virus. The term came from a Latin word meaning "slimy liquid, poison."

Vaccines are another way for our immune system to learn how to fight particular diseases. Vaccines are dead or weakened forms of bacteria and viruses. A doctor or other medical professional introduces these microorganisms into the body, either through an injection or in a drinkable dose. The body reacts just as it would to a stronger form of the infection. The immune system creates antibodies, and from that point on, the person usually is immune to that form of the disease.

Genetics

Heredity is the passing of characteristics from parents to a child. Genes are units of heredity that are passed down in our cells. They contain the instructions that make us who we are, from the color of our hair to health problems which we may experience. Each baby has a unique genetic code. That code stays the same as the baby grows into an adult, and until the end of his or her life.

Sometimes mutations in the genetic code cause rare diseases. These are not diseases anyone can catch from water or food or another person. People who have genetic diseases have them because that's the way their bodies are programmed.

A gene is the basic unit of heredity in a living thing. A genetic mutation can cause serious diseases and lead to other severe medical conditions.

PLAGUES

The Black Death, cholera, and smallpox are devastating diseases that have killed millions of people. Plagues like these have wiped out the populations of entire cities. Some plagues have traveled around the globe.

The Plague of Ashdod is an artist's representation of the Justinian Plague.

The Plague of Justinian

The Byzantine Empire, or East Roman Empire, was established by Emperor Constantinople in 330 CE and thrived until 1453 CE. But in 541 CE, when the empire was ruled by Emperor Justinian, a bacterial disease struck its capital, Constantinople.

Thousands of people died every day. One ancient record said that at one point there were ten thousand deaths per day. Eventually, 40 percent of the city's half million people had died. The plague continued to spread throughout the Byzantine Empire, killing 100 million people by the time it had run its course in 590 CE.

The Bubonic Plague (or, the Black Death)

This is probably the most well-known plague in history. Between 1347 and 1351, the bubonic plague killed 75 million people worldwide—25 million or more in Europe alone. Historians believe that the plague began in China and inner Asia and spread through the Mediterranean and into Europe.

The bubonic plague was bacterial. People developed buboes, or large blisters, that grew on their neck, armpits, and groin. The buboes were painful and oozed pus. People infected with the disease would begin vomiting and coughing up blood. They would usually die within a week's time.

INSIDE KNOWLEDGE

Yersinia pestis is the bacterium that causes bubonic plague. Rats carry this bacterium. The fleas that feast on rats then **transmit** the bacteria to humans. Although there are still nearly three thousand cases of bubonic plague reported every year, today's antibiotics are effective in treating the disease. The last major outbreak of bubonic plague in the United States was in Los Angeles from 1924 to 1925, but there are still one thousand to three thousand new cases every year.

Major European cities like London had two problems: too many rats, which carried the bacteria, and too many dead bodies to bury. Accounts from the time tell about the horrible stench in the streets from the bodies as well as from the rotting flesh of those who were still alive.

This illustration from an old manuscript shows plague victims in Perugia, Italy.

Typhoid, Cholera, and Deadly Water

During the 1800s, two diseases devastated Europe, Asia, and the Americas: cholera and typhoid. Both were caused mainly by bacteria in unsanitary water that people drank or used for preparing food.

Cholera was by far the more deadly of the two diseases. Its symptoms included violent vomiting and constant diarrhea. In major cities, the disease took hold because cities in the 1800s didn't have a system for dealing with sewage, especially human feces. Almost everything ran into the rivers and water supplies—especially in sections of cities where poor people lived.

Once the cholera bacterium got into the water supply, it began a vicious cycle of infection. People would get sick and their feces—which carried the bacterium—would be thrown back into the water supply. Then more people would drink the water and fall ill. Millions of people across the world died from the disease.

A polluted water supply could spread typhoid and cholera with frightening speed.

Typhoid spreads in the same way that cholera spreads—through contaminated water and food. The symptoms are also similar. Typhoid causes fevers as high as 104 degrees Fahrenheit (40 degrees Celsius). Eventually, it also leads to horrible diarrhea or severe constipation, and can cause internal bleeding. There are still outbreaks of typhoid today, but because sanitation has improved around the world, these occurrences are much smaller in scope. Scientists developed the first vaccine for the disease in 1896.

GENIUS AT WORK

Some consider John Snow to be the man who cured the cholera outbreak in London. In 1854, Dr. Snow began mapping where the disease was occurring. He saw that the cases in one of the poorer areas all seemed to be centered around a particular water pump. He convinced authorities to close down that pump. The number of cholera cases dropped almost immediately, proving that the water contained the source of the disease. Soon people began boiling water before using it and cholera came to a halt.

This is the original map made by John Snow in 1854. The outbreaks of cholera are shown in black. The location of the pump is circled.

Smallpox: Wiping Out a Deadly Disease

Smallpox was one of the deadliest of diseases, terrifying people for centuries. But today, it no longer exists. Smallpox was caused by a virus that is passed between people. Sneezing, coughing, kissing—even standing near someone with the virus could lead to infection. At first, the symptoms were like those of a cold: fever, headache, and muscle pain. But soon small pimplelike marks, called pustules, appeared on the skin. These pustules grew, hardened, and eventually faded, leaving scars all over peoples' skin—when they survived.

The smallpox virus now exists only in two laboratories in the United States and Russia—as far as anyone knows.

GENIUS AT WORK

Dr. Edward Jenner was a doctor and farmer living in rural England in the late 1700s. He noticed that the women who milked his cows weren't getting smallpox. These women did get a disease called cowpox, which was like smallpox but much milder and not fatal. Jenner wondered if giving people a small dose of cowpox could inoculate, or protect, them against smallpox. His idea worked. Jenner's cowpox experiment was one of the first known vaccines.

Records of smallpox outbreaks date back as far as 1350 BCE. European explorers brought the disease with them to North America in the 1500s and 1600s. The disease nearly wiped out Incan, Aztec, and American Indian populations. During the twentieth century alone, smallpox is thought to have killed at least 300 million people worldwide.

A global effort to vaccinate children against smallpox began in the 1950s. In 1980, the World Health Organization (WHO) declared that smallpox had been completely **eradicated**—the only disease that human science has been able to stop completely.

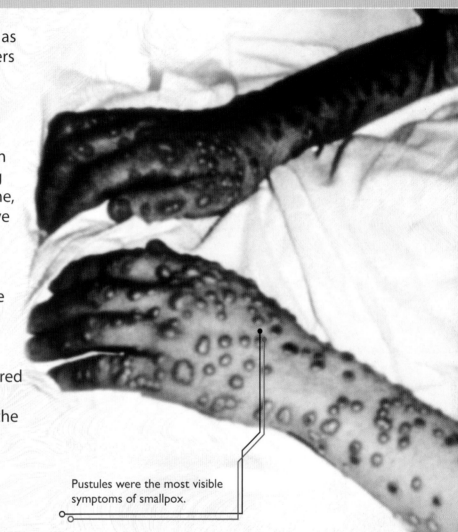

Pustules were the most visible symptoms of smallpox.

INSIDE KNOWLEDGE

Because of the fear of bioterrorism, the World Health Orgnaization (WHO) keeps the remaining samples of the smallpox virus in two laboratories, one in the United States and the other in Russia. The Centers for Disease Control in the United States has 451 samples of 229 different strains of the smallpox virus. Vector, part of the Institute of Molecular Biology in Russia, has 691 samples of 120 strains. At each storage location, the virus stocks are stored in liquid nitrogen freezers. They are also protected with complex security measures.

Malaria: Today's Plague

Malaria is an ancient disease. Something resembling it was described in Chinese medical writings around 2700 BCE. Today, malaria is found primarily in tropical regions in Asia, Africa, the Middle East, South America, and Central America. It affects more than 250 million people every year, killing about 900,000. The disease is transmitted from person to person by a familiar insect—the mosquito.

People get malaria from the bite of a female *Anopheles* mosquito. The mosquito bites a sick person and sucks a little blood containing the malarial parasite. Then it bites someone else and the infected blood enters that person's bloodstream. It takes between ten and twenty-eight days for the symptoms to appear: fever, chills, light-headedness, and nausea. If untreated, the person can go into a coma, or unconscious state. In severe cases, the person may even die. While there is no vaccine for malaria, today many drugs can help cure the disease.

A mosquito drinks infected blood from one person and then carries it to the next person it bites.

How Malaria Spreads

The parasite enters the body and infects the liver.

Blood passing through the liver is infected.

A mosquito carrying the malaria protozoan feeds on a person, called the host.

A second mosquito feeds on the host and carries infected blood to the next human.

Mosquitoes transmit infected blood from person to person.

Before scientists knew much about the causes of malaria, people understood that the sickness had something to do with swamps and standing water. In 1897, while stationed in India, British army doctor Ronald Ross let female mosquitoes feed on the blood of a man suffering from malaria. He found the malaria parasite in the stomach of one of these mosquitoes. Soon governments around the world were draining the swamps where mosquitoes bred and spraying them with mosquito-killing chemicals.

Inside Knowledge

What's the best way to prevent and treat malaria? UNICEF works with the World Health Organization (WHO) to raise money for the following materials:

- Netting treated with insecticides to cover beds while people sleep
- Clothes that cover as much of the skin as possible
- Mosquito-repelling creams and sprays
- Drugs to treat people who already have the disease

MORE PANDEMICS

Any infectious disease that spreads across large areas—a country, a continent, or the entire world—is called a pandemic. Plagues are pandemics.

It's not surprising that typhoid and malaria are considered pandemics. But one of the most common pandemic diseases is also one of the most familiar illnesses: the flu. The flus that make the headlines, though, are very different from the ones that keep us home in bed for a day or two.

In 1918, this emergency hospital was set up at Camp Funston, Kansas, to help deal with the influenza epidemic.

Spread of the Spanish Flu

Influenza, or the flu, is caused by a virus. Because viruses can mutate, it's very hard for scientists and doctors to find a cure. In 1918 and 1919, a particular strain of flu killed more than 25 million people worldwide. (Some estimates even say 50 million, or 3 percent of the world's population, died from it.) Called the Spanish Influenza, this pandemic actually is thought to have begun in a U.S. army camp in Kansas. Soldiers shipped off to Europe during World War I brought the disease with them. Other soldiers caught it and returned to their homes all around the world.

By the summer of 1918, the Spanish flu began spreading like wildfire. In Massachusetts, within two weeks of the first people falling ill, thousands of new cases were also reported. Most people died of pneumonia that accompanied the flu. (Pneumonia is a condition in which the lungs hold water and become swollen.) Many died within two days of getting the disease.

Flyers like this were posted in an attempt to help stop the spread of the Spanish flu.

INSIDE KNOWLEDGE

The Spanish flu got its name because Spain's news was not censored during World War I. So, more news stories about the pandemic came from Spain than from anywhere else. This gave the impression that Spain was the center of this deadly disease.

Scientists now believe that the virus that caused the Spanish flu pandemic was an H1N1 virus, a very powerful virus that mutates quickly. This is the same strain of virus that created huge concerns beginning in 2008 as it spread to different parts of the world.

EPIDEMIC INFLUENZA (SPANISH)

This Disease is Highly Communicable. It May Develop Into a Severe Pneumonia.

There is no medicine which will prevent it.

Keep away from public meetings, theatres and other places where crowds are assembled.

Keep the mouth and nose covered while coughing or sneezing.

When a member of the household becomes ill, place him in a room by himself. The room should be warm, but well ventilated.

The attendant should put on a mask before entering the room of those ill of the disease.

TO MAKE A MASK

Take a piece of ordinary cheesecloth 8 x 16 inches, fold it to make it 8 x 8 inches. Next fold this to make it 8 x 4 inches. Tie cords about 10 inches long at each corner. Apply over mouth and nose as shown in the picture.

ISSUED BY THE PROVINCIAL BOARD OF HEALTH

Tuberculosis: An Ancient Disease

Tuberculosis (TB) is an ancient illness—so ancient that it has actually been found in Egyptian mummies! Tuberculosis is a bacterial disease. It is spread from person to person through the air by coughing, sneezing, or even talking. The bacteria get into the lungs and create thick masses that destroy lung tissue. For people with tuberculosis, breathing becomes harder and harder as their lungs are destroyed. They often begin to cough up blood.

Tuberculosis hit industrial cities hard during the late 1800s and early 1900s. Millions of people around the world died from the disease. Patients were often sent to **sanatoriums**, which isolated those suffering from the disease and gave them a chance to get better—if they were lucky. In 1921, two French scientists invented an effective vaccine for tuberculosis. For the next sixty years, the number of people developing tuberculosis fell dramatically. But in recent years, the disease has made a comeback in developing countries. According to the Centers for Disease Control and Prevention, one third of the world's population is infected with TB.

A woman in Ethiopia receives medicine to help battle tuberculosis.

Destroying Polio

Polio is a viral disease that attacks the nervous system, specifically the spinal cord. This can cause permanent damage to leg, arm, and other body muscles. People are sometimes paralyzed. Most of those struck with polio are young children. It is spread from person to person through unwashed hands or contaminated food or water.

It wasn't until the late 1800s that polio became a widespread problem. But then it became worse and worse. In 1917, 9,000 children were diagnosed with the disease in New York City alone and 2,400 died from it. There is no cure for polio, but in 1955, a new vaccine was introduced to fight the spread of the disease. Since then, polio has been virtually wiped out in the United States and other countries with broad access to the vaccine. But one thousand to two thousand children, most of them in India, are still paralyzed by polio each year.

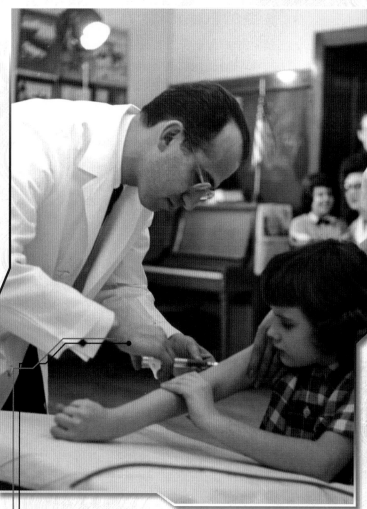

Dr. Jonas Salk developed a polio vaccine that nearly eliminated the disease.

Just Amazing!

In the early stages of polio, some people were unable even to breathe on their own. Many died. Then, in 1927, Philip Drinker and Louis Agassiz Shaw at Harvard University devised a special tank. The tank had a motor and vacuum pumps that kept changing the air pressure within, pulling air in and out of the lungs. These "tank respirators" became known as iron lungs. They kept patients alive until they could again breathe on their own.

Ebola: Fast and Deadly

Deadly diseases are not just "old news." Several new ones have surfaced in recent decades. Ebola is a virus that is very infectious. It was first identified in 1976 in Africa in the Republic of Congo near the Ebola River. This is a horrible disease: people begin to bleed inside their body, and eventually blood finds its way out of every opening. Ebola can cause death in eight to seventeen days.

The Ebola virus is so deadly that the patient must be isolated, and doctors must work in protective suits.

The Ebola virus shocked Africans and eventually the world. Because the virus is so strong and so deadly, scientists must be completely protected and covered in sealed plastic suits just to study the disease. It is unclear where the virus came from. That means there is still no cure and no vaccine. Still, international health organizations have done a great deal to keep the disease from spreading worldwide. They locate outbreaks quickly, and put safeguards in to stop the spread into neighboring communities.

HIV/AIDS: A Modern Plague?

In 1980, scientists realized that a new and frightening disease had begun killing people around the world. AIDS—acquired immune deficiency syndrome—has killed more than 25 million people worldwide since the epidemic began. The cause of AIDS is the HIV virus, which breaks down the immune system. This leaves those with AIDS unable to fight off germs that most of us can handle easily.

Over the years, a variety of drugs have been created to slow the progress of HIV. With treatment, many people with AIDS have lived long, healthy lives once the disease has been diagnosed. While no cure yet exists, in 2009 a clinical trial of a new vaccine showed some promise.

People with AIDS who aren't taking medication develop damaged areas of the skin, called lesions, all over their body.

INSIDE KNOWLEDGE

No one can say for sure where HIV/AIDS originated, but the strongest scientific theory is that it first arose in Africa among certain chimpanzees. HIV is closely related to a virus found in these chimps. The theory is that hunters may have been bitten by these chimps or may even have eaten them.

Flu in Flight

In the last ten years or so, a few influenza viruses have threatened to become pandemics. In 1997, a strange flu broke out in Hong Kong, one of the world's most populated cities. Called the avian flu (or bird flu), it was carried by birds—specifically chickens, ducks, and geese—and passed on to humans. Only a small number of people died from the virus. But scientists worldwide were worried about geese flying from country to country and infecting other birds. They also worried about chickens, which are shipped around the world. The government in Hong Kong slaughtered every chicken it could find—more than a million. A bird flu vaccine was finally developed in 2007.

To prevent the spread of avian flu, farmers and government agencies killed millions of chickens suspected of carrying the virus.

West Nile Virus

In 1999, a strange virus was found in a small number of people and a large number of birds in the Bronx Zoo in New York. What was surprising was that the virus was identified as the West Nile virus—usually found in Africa and the Middle East. By 2002, the virus had spread across the United States. More than six hundred people had died from the virus, which causes swelling in the brain. The virus was spread by mosquitoes. The West Nile virus hasn't reached pandemic levels in the United States. Still, every mosquito season brings the chance that the virus will mutate into an even deadlier strain.

The transmission of swine flu from pigs to humans is believed to take place primarily on swine farms, where people are in constant contact with the animals.

Swine Flu Outbreak

In 2009, the United States was hit with an outbreak of the H1N1 virus, also known as swine flu. (Although the virus is found in pigs, scientists have since learned that eating pork products does not lead to the flu.) H1N1 is a powerful strain of flu that is very contagious. In only a few months, hundreds of children died from swine flu. Nearly fifteen thousand people have died from it around the world, which makes it a pandemic. When the danger of the flu became clear, the U.S. government made a huge effort to create millions of doses of a new vaccine for the virus. Governments are still working hard to control the spread of the disease.

DISEASES OF THE SKIN

Our skin is our largest organ—no wonder there are so many ways it can be infected!

Common skin problems, like acne or rashes, are annoying but easily treatable. But there are some skin diseases that are very rare. Some can be cured, some cannot, and some can even cause death.

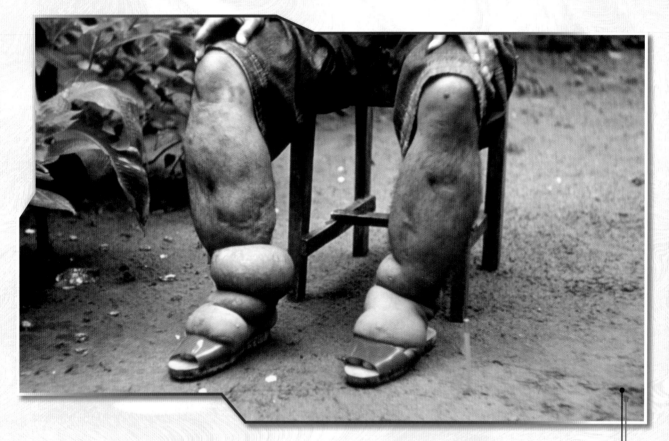

Elephantiasis: Too Much Skin

Elephantiasis is a disease that is found mostly in tropical regions, especially in Africa, South America, and Asia. The disease is caused by two parasites: roundworms and mosquitoes. The roundworm carries the disease, and the mosquitoes transfer it from the worm to humans.

Elephantiasis causes gross enlargement of limbs, and sometimes of the head or other areas of the body.

The infection causes a blockage of the body's lymphatic system. This system is a network of channels and organs that helps maintain proper fluid levels in the body. The blockage leads to massive swelling of the skin and underlying tissue, especially of the legs and arms. Those who get the disease end up having lots of extra sagging skin that looks something like the skin of an elephant.

It is estimated that 120 million people worldwide suffer from a form of this disease, and those numbers are growing. Elephantiasis isn't deadly, and there are antibiotics that can help treat the disease. But the skin and tissue are permanently damaged. There is no vaccine yet for elephantiasis. However, a drug called diethylcarbamazine is showing some promise in treating people in the early stages of the disease.

Inside Knowledge

England's Joseph Merrick was known as "The Elephant Man." He became world famous in the late 1800s because of the strange disease that made parts of his body look like he had elephant skin. He worked as a circus freak before a doctor discovered him and wanted to study the causes and symptoms. Historians have assumed Merrick suffered from elephantiasis. But DNA research shows that he probably had a very different genetic disease that caused the tissue in his body to grow abnormally thick. Merrick died in his sleep at age twenty-seven. He had always slept sitting up. Doctors believe that when he decided to try to sleep lying down, as most people do, the weight of his head tightened his throat and caused him to suffocate.

Leprosy: Centuries of Shame

Leprosy has existed for about four thousand years. It is a bacterial disease that can take as long as twenty years to become visible. People with leprosy develop lesions, or hard pimplelike bumps, on their face, arms, and legs. Nerves in the surrounding areas are destroyed. Luckily, only about 5 percent of people who get infected actually develop the disease. Most people have immune systems that are able to fight off the bacterium that causes leprosy.

In ancient times, when the disease was not treatable, the lesions could be so bad and go so deep into the body that fingers, toes, and noses fell off. This caused such fear in others that people with leprosy often became outcasts.

A woman waits in a leprosy hospital in Karachi, Pakistan.

Leprosy Today

These statistics from the World Health Organization show that there are still many new cases of leprosy.

WHO Region	Number of New Cases, 2008
Southeast Asia	120,967
The Americas	49,388
Africa	30,055
Western Pacific	8,152
Eastern Mediterranean	4,240

In 1873, a Norwegian scientist named G. H. Hansen discovered the bacterium that causes leprosy. (The disease is now called Hansen's disease.) Since then, researchers have found a treatment called multidrug therapy (MDT) that can be used to treat and cure leprosy. Still, it is a tough bacterium: more than 200,000 new cases still arise every year.

JUST AMAZING

The story of leprosy is more about fear than science. In the past, "lepers" were treated as objects of terror and isolated from so-called healthy, or uninfected, people. Every country in the world had "leper colonies"—some were even on separate islands. In the United States, there was one leper colony—Carville, in Louisiana—that used barbed wire to keep those with leprosy inside. Today we know that the disease is not easy to pass from person to person. There was no reason to isolate those with leprosy.

The Reverend Billy Graham visits a "leper colony" in Nigeria, in 1960. At the time, few people would risk going near those who had the disease.

Flesh-Eating Disease

The official name of this bacterial disease is necrotizing fasciitis, but the more familiar name is flesh-eating disease. This is a very dangerous disease that can lead to death if not treated. About 50 percent of the people who get a flesh-eating disease die from it.

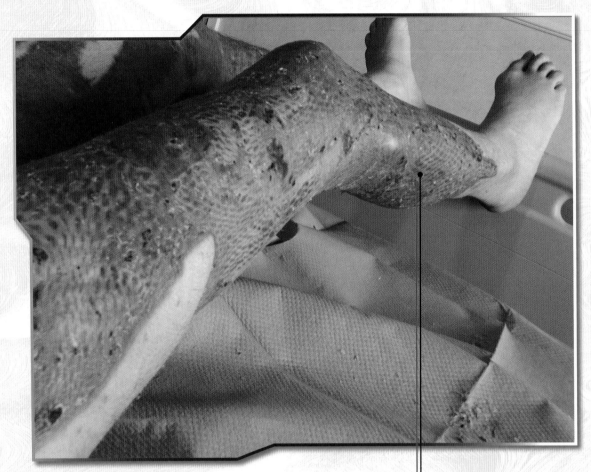

This bacterium works fast. It gets into the human body through a cut or scrape, or through the **mucous membranes.** Within forty-eight hours, blisters form around the red, inflamed cut. The disease is extremely painful. In fact, horrible pain from what looks like a simple infected cut is one clue that a person might have this disease. The damage is being done underneath the skin.

The flesh-eating disease spreads rapidly and is often fatal.

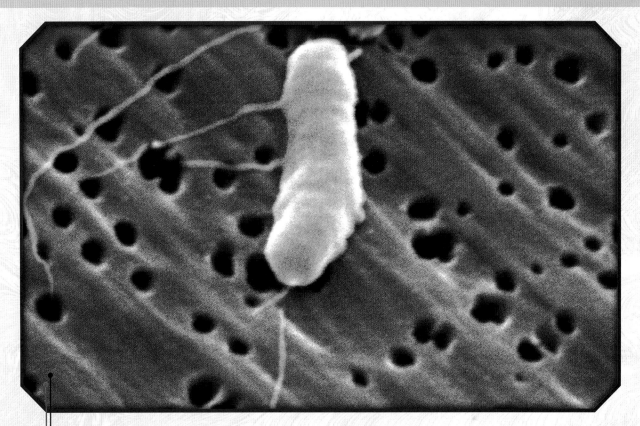

The flesh-eating bacterium doesn't actually eat anything. It releases poisons that destroy skin, muscle, and tissue.

Surgery is necessary to stop the spread of necrotizing fasciitis. Otherwise, bacteria will continue to infect tissue and muscle rapidly. Surgeons pull up the skin where the bacteria are working and cut out the infected tissue. This can mean cutting away large amounts of tissue, depending on how far the disease has spread. In extreme cases, the entire arm or leg has to be amputated.

INSIDE KNOWLEDGE

The name flesh-eating disease is a bit of an exaggeration. The bacterium doesn't actually eat anything. It releases toxins, or poisons, that destroy skin, muscle, and tissue. But these toxins are powerful and fast-acting. The most common bacterium that causes necrotizing fasciitis is a dangerous form of streptococcus. You may have heard the word in relation to strep throat. This is a throat infection caused by the same bacterium as the one that causes flesh-eating disease. Luckily, it is not nearly as dangerous.

UNAUSUAL GENETIC DISEASES

Most diseases are caused by outside agents like bacteria and viruses. There are some, though, that have nothing to do with the world around us. Some are built into our genetic codes.

Genes: Human Instruction Codes

Each person has a unique genetic code. The code is your DNA. You get one set of instructions from your mother and one set from your father. These two combine to make your DNA code. In some people, the two sets of instructions don't combine quite right. One part of the code can be slightly off, or mutated. These mutations can sometime lead to rare, and sometimes bizarre, diseases.

DNA carries the hereditary information in humans and almost all other organisms.

JUST AMAZING!

DNA molecules are made up of repeating units called nucleotides. These nucleotides appear in base pairs that form each "rung" of the DNA ladder. Although the pairs themselves are very small, the longest DNA molecule in the human body is 220 million base pairs long!

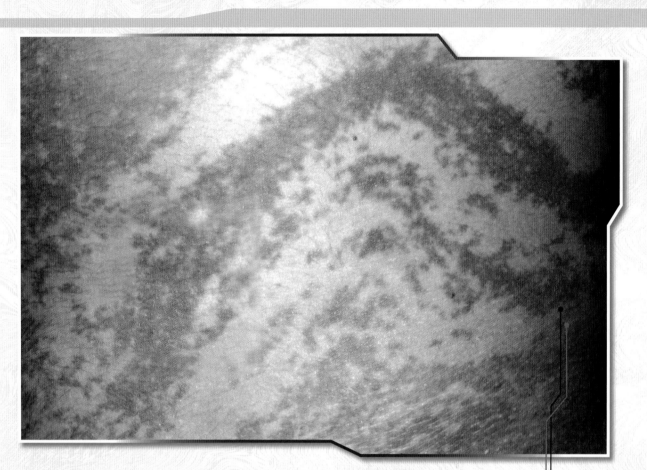

Everyone has Blaschko's lines, but on most people they are invisible.

Striped Like a Tiger

Blaschko's lines are lines on the skin that can't be seen under normal conditions. But several diseases cause these lines to become visible. V- shaped and swirling patterns appear. Sometimes, too, people inherit two sets of DNA that don't match up correctly.

In that case, one set of DNA instructions calls for lighter or darker skin than the other. These differences show up along Blaschko's lines.

INSIDE KNOWLEDGE

Blaschko's lines are thought by many to show the growth and movement of skin cells during the development of the fetus. They are V-shaped on the upper spine, S-shaped on the abdomen, an inverted U-shape from the chest area to the upper arm, and perpendicular down the front and back of the lower arms and legs.

Progeria: Too Old Too Fast

All kids want to grow up and do the things adults can do. But for children born with the rare genetic disease called progeria, time moves tragically fast.

This very rare disease causes children to start aging quickly—as soon as they are born.

Fransie Geringer was only eleven years old when this picture was taken.

Symptoms of progeria include:

- Growth failure during the first year of life
- Narrow, shrunken, or wrinkled face
- Baldness
- Loss of eyebrows and eyelashes
- Shortness
- Large head for size of face
- Open soft spot on head
- Small jaw
- Dry, scaly, thin skin
- Limited range of motion
- Teeth—delayed or absent

Most children born with progeria never get any taller than the average five year old. They still act like children, but they look like much older people, with wrinkled skin and very little or no hair. Inside, their bodies are also aging quickly: their bones get fragile, and they start to have problems with their heart. Interestingly, the disease doesn't seem to affect their brains—they think like kids and they don't have the memory loss problems that trouble many elderly people.

The genetic mutation that causes progeria is located in one tiny spot of the DNA of those affected. There is no cure for it, and no way to prevent it. Most people with progeria don't live past the age of thirteen. Since 1886, there have only been about 130 recorded cases of the disease.

This old photo is one of the only remaining images of the Fugate family. Notice that not every family member had blue skin. Only those who received the gene from both the mother and the father developed that characteristic.

JUST AMAZING!

The Fugate family of Troublesome Creek, Kentucky, had blue skin. Really. (And that's really the real name of their town, too.) The family moved to Kentucky in the early 1800s. Many family members married people from another nearby family. At it turned out, both families carried a rare code on their DNA that matched up and made their babies' skin turn blue. This trait was passed on from generation to generation for 150 years. The disease didn't cause any health problems—just blue skin. In fact, many family members lived well into their eighties.

Abys DeJesus was born with thick facial hair and lived mostly indoors. A Phildadelphia surgeon found a way to graft healthy skin over the affected area.

Howling at the Moon?

Werewolves are just imaginary characters in books and horror movies, right? Yes, but there is a rare genetic disease that causes extreme hair growth all over the body: hypertrichosis, often called Human Werewolf Syndrome. When a person has this disease, thick hair grows all over the face. This happens even to women and children. Throughout history, people with Werewolf Syndrome, such as "the Bearded Woman" or "the Wolf Boy," took jobs in circuses as sideshow attractions. There's no cure for the disease, but there are many ways for people to have hair removed permanently.

JUST AMAZING!

If you know your vampire lore, you know those imaginary creatures are sensitive to light and can't be exposed to the sun. That's where Vampire Disease gets its name. It's actually a form of a disease called porphyria, which affects the blood, skin, and nervous system. One version of this genetic disease causes the skin to blister in the sun. It can also affect the gums and cause itching and decay of the skin. Other forms of porphyria attack internal organs. But it's the sensitivity to light that connects the disease to the myth of vampires.

Straight-Faced

Imagine talking to someone whose face never moves, who never smiles or shows surprise, and who never even blinks. This is called Möbius Syndrome, an extremely rare genetic disease with no known cure. Because of a genetic mutation, the muscles and nerves in the faces of people with Möbius Syndrome don't work right. No matter what emotion the person is feeling, his or her face simply cannot respond. Most people with Möbius Syndrome live normal lives. Since they can't blink, though, they have to use special eye drops to keep their eyeballs from drying out.

This man may be feeling happy, but because of Möbius Syndrome, his face cannot show any expression.

BIOTERRORISM

Diseases can be frightening enough when they happen naturally. But throughout history, people have also used them as a way to destroy their enemies.

There's a story that Europeans who settled in America in the 1500s and 1600s gave American Indians blankets infected with smallpox in order to kill entire tribes. Although there is no evidence that this actually happened, there are letters from a British Army officer in 1763 suggesting this idea.

But even if this one British officer didn't use disease as a weapon, other people have. This type of warfare is known as bioterrorism—the purposeful use of viruses, bacteria, or other disease toxins to infect or kill thousands of people all at once. Bioterrorism has been around for centuries. But because of the advances in weaponry and science over the past one hundred years, the threat of such an attack is even more frightening.

Anthrax is a deadly infectious disease caused by these spore-forming bacteria. It is often used in biological warfare.

Outlawing Bioterrorism

Over the centuries, countries have created more and more deadly biological weapons. Because of the awful effects of the chemical mustard gas used during World War I, a treaty was signed in 1925 that outlawed the use of chemical and biological weapons in wartime. In 1972, the Biological and Toxin Weapons Convention banned the creation or stockpiling of biological and chemical weapons. Most countries have signed the convention, but some still have not.

Just Amazing!

In the 1300s, in what is now Ukraine, the Mongols used bioterrorism in battle. Historians believe it was one of the reasons the bubonic plague spread throughout Europe. The Mongols were attacking the city of Caffa. They used catapults to hurl hundreds of diseased dead bodies inside the city walls. As people fled the city, many of them were already infected and brought the plague to different cities in Europe.

Gas masks may be used to protect against biological terrorism.

Controlling Deadly Diseases

Many countries still fear biological attacks from others, so they keep strains of the diseases warehoused—just in case. Because diseases like smallpox or anthrax pose a great threat to people, these samples are closely guarded. The following are some of the most feared diseases that could result from a bioterrorism attack:

- **Pneumonic Plague**: This is another version of the bubonic plague, only this can be passed through the air. A weapon of bioterrorism that sprays the bacteria for this disease could be inhaled by thousands of people in one attack, resulting in many deaths.

- **Smallpox**: Although this viral disease has been wiped out worldwide, there are still samples housed in laboratories in Russia and the United States. Because smallpox spreads so easily from person to person, a biological terror attack could infect hundreds of thousands of people very quickly.

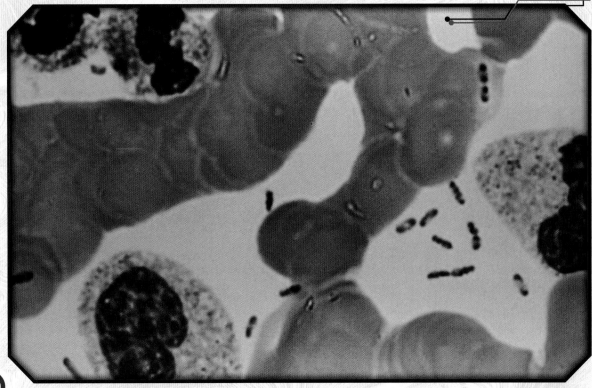

Dark-stained bacteria are seen here attacking blood cells in a plague victim.

- **Ebola**: Since Ebola is a fast-acting and very deadly virus, an attack using Ebola could kill large numbers of people very quickly. Because the virus is still found in regions of Africa, the fear is that a terrorist group could create a weapon using it.

- **Anthrax**: In order for people to get anthrax, the bacteria must be inhaled or ingested (eaten or swallowed). Because it can be inhaled, a bioterrorist attack could infect thousands of people quickly. Anthrax isn't contagious, though, and there are antibiotics that will cure it if they are used quickly.

Biohazard signs like this one may be used to warn people of the presence of dangerous bacteria or viruses.

INSIDE KNOWLEDGE

The only known bioterrorism attack on America happened in the fall of 2001, not long after the terrorist attack of September 11. Some members of Congress and the media received envelopes containing anthrax. They were sent through the U.S. mail. Five people died as a result of inhaling the anthrax spores. At the time, the fear of another bioterrorism attack was high. Luckily, there hasn't been another such attack in the United States.

Disease Control and Prevention

The most effective ways to deal with all kinds of diseases are preparation and prevention. The U.S. Centers for Disease Control and Prevention (CDC) make up one of the world's best organizations for dealing with disease.

The Malaria Zone

The CDC was founded in Atlanta, Georgia, in 1946. At the time there was a huge outbreak of malaria in the southeast. The CDC's initial focus was on figuring out ways to kill mosquitoes, the parasite that carries malaria. As time went on, it became important for the United States to have a first-rate agency that could track diseases around the country, research cures and vaccines, and educate the public about all kinds of health issues.

This facility is part of the Centers for Disease Control and Prevention in Atlanta, Georgia.

To remain safe, this scientist wears a self-contained suit as he examines poisonous material.

Genius at Work

How valuable are the scientists at the CDC? In 2009, during the swine flu scare, the CDC tracked all reported cases around the country. They quickly identified the virus—H1N1—and sent out public health warnings about how to prevent the spread of the disease. The CDC also worked with the government and drug manufacturers to develop a vaccine for swine flu in record time.

One thing the CDC does is act as a central information hub for health and disease information. When doctors encounter unusual diseases or illnesses, they report it to the CDC. The organization then keeps track of when and where diseases occur. The CDC also does important research.

Acting as "disease detectives," scientists at the CDC learn about, cure, and prevent all kinds of illnesses. The library of information at the CDC is amazing. Doctors and public health officials from all around the country—and the world—use the CDC's knowledge to help identify and treat diseases. Thanks to the CDC and its partner organizations, the world becomes a bit safer each day.

GLOSSARY

antibodies Proteins developed by the body to fight off harmful substances.

dysentery An infection that causes severe diarrhea.

eradicate To get rid of completely.

genetic defect A mutation, or permanent change, in the genetic code of a person or animal.

immune system The body's system for protecting against disease and illnesses.

microorganisms Tiny one-celled organisms; especially viruses, fungi, and bacteria.

molecules Tiny particles made up of atoms.

mucous membranes A thin tissue lining below the skin, as in the nose and mouth.

nausea Feeling sick to one's stomach.

pharmacies Places where medicine and prescriptions are dispensed.

respiratory Dealing with the lungs and breathing.

ringworm Fungus disease with ring-shaped patches on the skin.

sanatorium A place to isolate and treat contagious patients.

sleeping sickness Tropical disease carried by flies; causes extreme sleepiness.

transmit To pass from one person to another.

FIND OUT MORE

Books

Arnold, Nick, and Tony De Saulles. *Deadly Diseases and Microscopic Monsters*. New York: Scholastic, 2009. Readers will discover how tiny bacteria and viruses can destroy the human body.

Peters, Stephanie T. *The Battle Against Polio*. New York: Marshall Cavendish Benchmark, 2004. Explores the effects of this disease on the world.

Tilden, Thomasine E. Lewis. *Help! What's Eating My Flesh?: Runaway Staph and Strep Infections!* New York: Scholastic, 2007. Bacteria are everywhere, and this colorful book provides highly accessible facts and information about some of the strangest bacterial diseases—and how to protect yourself from them.

Websites

www.bam.gov
BAM stands for Body and Mind, a great site created by the Centers for Disease Control. A special section on diseases provides information on the latest infections and how to combat them.

http://kidshealth.org/teen/your_body/health_basics/genes_genetic_disorders.html
A good site for learning the basics of genetics and how genetic disorders and mutations occur.

INDEX